41-10134

POEMS · RIDGELY TORRENCE

THE MACMILLAN COMPANY
NEW YORK · BOSTON · CHICAGO
DALLAS · ATLANTA · SAN FRANCISCO

MACMILLAN AND CO., LIMITED
LONDON · BOMBAY · CALCUTTA
MADRAS · MELBOURNE

THE MACMILLAN COMPANY
OF CANADA, LIMITED
TORONTO

POEMS

By

RIDGELY
TORRENCE

THE MACMILLAN COMPANY
NEW YORK · 1941

TO

LOUIS V. LEDOUX

CONTENTS

TO CHILDREN

POEMS

LIGHT

Not this light, not the lightfall on earth, on sea
or on meadow,
But the light at light's heart, the unfading, the
light without shadow.

Not this air, not this earth, not this love, hope,
sorrow and rapture,
Not these moons, hours, faces and dreams which
none may recapture.

But where is full day? And clear vision? And how
far to find,
Overarching, unbroken, the sky yielding sight to
the blind?

And who knows if the living are there, if such
healings are shed,

Or if somewhere in fullness it blazes, but over the
dead?

And where, near by or far off, or under what
dome
Is the great good place? Is there any? Sure harbor
and home?

Yes, this light that falls in the darkness on land
and sea meadow,
This broken, this exile splendor that wanders in
shadow.

Yes this earth, yes this hope, yes this love, joy and
grief for the lover,
Yes these orbs, hours, faces, these dreams that a
dream may recover.

Here clouded, forever half-lost between triumph
and doom

Night-islanded life, unquenched, slowly widens
its room

With beacons, with dawns that unveil it, the
hidden and strange,
As it lifts from the steadfast tides of the ocean of
change,

With rays on footholds gaining to summits more
proud
And won more surely than under a sky without
cloud,

And better than any escape to a sky apart
Are gleams from the heights to the shadows that
lie in the heart.

EUROPA AND THE BULL

(In this hour)

Strayed from what meadow of hell this
    bellowing shape
To her who sees the figures of her dread
Stem from the belly and from out the head
And sees the hooves beneath the lowered nape
Plunge, as she seeks in earth and sky, escape?
But he shall reach her where her steps have led
And we shall see, from earth and overhead,
Her fainting glories galloped to the rape.

And when the seed of this has sprung up armed,
Half beast, all monster, swift to bring about
Its battles for the coming of the dark,
Whoever lives and still has eyes unharmed
May see at last those hoof-like feet stamp out
The torch of mind, man's dream, to the last
    spark.

MEN AND WHEAT

Men march in the harvest heat
  Past fields to the fife's thin cry.
The men can see the wheat
  Wave, as the ranks go by.

They see the ripened yield
  Who'll never reap the grain;
They march to another field
  Where they shall leave the slain.

The wheat shall be next year's bread
  When rain has mixed with mire
The men with the flag ahead
  And the fifer's ditty of fire.

The sheaves of men lie flat
  And are buried where they bleed.
But what dread food is that?
  And what mouths does it feed?

ON STORM KING EDGE

Bright glow the worlds tonight, through frost,
    through fire,
  Far overhead above the meadow.
Light seems their dance through ether's halls,
  Dark the way of earth in shadow.

Is earth's way dark? Then darker, darker far
  Are ways that turn aside from pity;
The ways of those who take the sword
  And on the victim build their city.

Lampless the walls, venomed the lands that once
  Flowered with the free who kept and
    nourished,
In hope of fruit, the seed of peace.
  Now silence falls where music flourished.

Look to the land that bore us. Know from these
  Its leaf may fade, its flower may sicken
And bindweed spring among the roots
  And seeds from fields of fury quicken.

LINCOLN'S DREAM

Before dawn, Good Friday, April 14th, 1865

How can I tell them what it was I saw
When none of them were with me in that world?
I was alone and always am alone.
No one from earth was with me in the dream,
On the dark ship again tonight bound outward.
Or in that other dream twelve nights ago
When, with the peace assured, I slept at last,
Then seemed to wake, roused by the sound of
      mourning
Here in the White House, and to find it empty,
To meet with no one that the eye could see
As I went searching, till I reached a thing
Not to be shared with others till its hour.
There in the East Room, waiting, there it was:
The mourners and the silence and the soldiers.
The unearthly funeral light that blazed from
      nowhere.

The high-raised catafalque. The Form that lay
      there
With the face covered. Hid. But not from me.
I knew it. Who knew better? There I lay.
"The President is dead." No need to say so.
Though the loud burst of grief that swept the
      dream
Moved me to want to tell it. But to whom?
Who, of the multitudes that walk in daylight,
Has understood when I have told my dreams?
They lack the gift or curse of having eyes
Or visions such as mine, that I had always,
Bloody presentments, shapes of fear and doom
That seemed to hint my kinship with the shades,
Even as a baby, staring through the chinks
At the red mists between me and the stars.
—"Bawn to see evil," old black Sam would say.

And afterwards, before I learned to read,
The grandeurs and the glooms that came about
      me

When fever burned the veils before me

     thinner . . .

The cities seen before I ever reached them . . .

The worlds and faces boiling up from darkness

At night, in mother's time . . . "There, who's that,

     mother?

What's the man saying?" "What man?" "With

     the dagger."

"Why, Abe, there's no one there. You're seeing

     ghosts."

And so I was. And I have seen them since

And not less real than anything on earth

Seen with the outward eye lighted by reason.

We pioneers are superstitious people;

We live so near the edge of the unknown.

Though, if we see too much there, we can always

Look outward and fall back on common sense.

The line's as narrow as a razor edge

Between a mind well lighted and the darkness.

But what I've seen, I've seen. High noon's no

     clearer.

Daylight has yielded sight, as well as darkness.
For I was broad awake when I saw plain
My double image in the glass at Springfield,
One face alive, the other—not the same,
A thing to turn away from as I did.
And both reflected me. I knew its meaning:
The living face foretold my four years here,
The other—what's to come. I shudder at it,
But never for myself.

                       There's something else.
I've worn through every fear now but the worst,
Only to find it growing in my sleep,
Shaped in my vision of the shadowy ship.
Ten times I've dreamed it and again tonight,
Even in my broken rest, finding myself
Once more on board that dim, mysterious deck,
Fixed like a part of it and sensing only
Darkness, the hid wheel and the helmsman hidden
And prow set into darkness as the ship

Moves with a giant force through the dark water,
Swift to an unknown shore. And by what star?
What is the ship? What passengers, what cargoes
Are gathered in that hold? I guess and fear
The portent, that the vessel in the dream
May be the brave and danger-blind republic
Marked for a further grief soon to be suffered.
What if some new blow threatens her and the
      dream
Comes as a sad foretelling? This may be.
I see it always like a shadow cast
Before some great event. And though it often
Presages some right triumph, yet not always.
For it appeared before our victories,
Antietam, Gettysburg,—but in the end
What did those victories cost us? Young men
      dead.
Dead. On both sides. The nation's life. The
      flower.
And in a war that never would have been

But for blind pilots long before it struck.

So with all wars; there never yet was one

That might not, with clear vision and just action,

Have been avoided and the storm dissolved.

Yes, the republic lives. But for how long?

How long will she pursue through darkening seas

The free, unfearing course her builders laid?

What sorrows wait for her beyond the sea line?

What hidden shoals? What perils of the shallows?

Or from the bottom when the earthquakes come

Pushing up peaks with fangs unknown before?

Will she go down? Or some earth-rocking wave

Wash her free glories on far shores, to lie

Manacled on the rocks, bare to the keel

That should have kept home harbor in the storm?

Or will she ride the deluge and then drift

Slowly to some Sargasso and lie there

And in the fat backwaters grope for comfort

Through the dry rot of never setting sail,

Rusting in fears, tangled in idle calms,

Never to dare new seas or hardier ways?

But beyond all that threatens, all that strikes,
Whatever shadows, bolts, disasters, dooms
Loom from the sea or air to bring her down,
None are so dangerous as those within,
Nursed in her freedom, suffered to be here,
A thousand evils, that we may be free
Of the one greater which would make us slaves.
So it will be with every state that sails
True to the free and democratic course;
The hardest of all paths to steer upon,
The easiest assailed, yet, in the end,
The only forward track. Which, being lost,
Must then, however late, be found and followed
And all begun again. Though dangers ride
Aboard this nation, she has carried danger
Since first the seas embraced her and she stood
Free to whatever winds the sky could send,
And sailed, as now, with hazards that could sink
        her.

With the self-seekers and the backward-turners
Who fought to shape her course as in these days.
With folly-chosen captains, then as now,
Swayed by the brainless will of those who place
     them.
With wrongs, with pilots who would sail astray
And with blind borers hollowing out the frame.
With blazing envies, hatreds that may spread
And with their sea-fires burn her to the ocean.
All these she carries and is still afloat.
I trust the people as I trust the stars.
And if they lose the reckoning they will find it,
For they must learn and by their griefs they will,
Must learn to steer themselves, steer or be
     steered.
And if they lose their freedom they will find it
And, lost for times enough, they'll learn to keep
     it.
They've come this far and they have weathered
     all
But what's to come.

Or is the vision larger
And the dark ship the earth, or life itself?
If so, these fears will have an end at last,
One with the breast that held them, as the vessel
Gathers my littleness and all its pain
Into that hold that bore me to this place
And with dark pointing takes me away again,
Perhaps to further shores or to some vastness
Where there may still be dawns or perhaps
        darkness.
But beyond that, there may be other dreams.

Is that you, John? I'm waiting for a message.
You're up too late, or early. Night's for sleep.
Boy, go lie down. I'll watch. It's not yet day.

HARVEST HOME

Leave the thirsting cattle,
  Leave the standing grain,
Go and win the battle,
  Go and heap the slain.

That's the daring labor
  For the richer yield:
Neighbor reaping neighbor
  In the trampled field.

Reap with will to bind it.
  Reap through flesh and bone.
Find the life behind it,
  Reaper, is your own.

When the foe is scattered,
  Time will heap the cost,
And the victor, shattered,
  Know that he has lost.

ADAM'S DYING

He dreamed first
  Of what seem
The things worst
  In the dream:

The lost bower,
  The grave's drouth,
The sword's power,
  The worm's mouth.

He dreamed last
  Of good things:
The pain past,
  The air's wings.

The seed furled,
  The stirred dust,
Sight's world,
  The hand's thrust.

Thought's birth,
  The mind's blade,

27

Work's worth,
  The thing made.

The wind's haste,
  The cloud's dove,
The fruit's taste,
  The heart's love.

The sky's dome,
  The sun's west,
A man's home,
  Eve's breast.

The wave's beach,
  The bird's wood,
Dreams, each,
  But all good.

Life finds rest
  Where life rose.
Which was best?
  The heart knows.

THE WATCHER

The gemlike eyes for sight,
  The vision that lights the being,
The glories of day and night
  That wait the glory of seeing,

All these will not avail
  Against that blinding power
Before whose glare grow pale
  All hues of flesh and flower,

Against the doom to which
  The nations rush, divided,
And leave the furrows rich,
  Fear-fevered, folly-guided,

To that which waits to grind
  The reaping with the reaper,
Which looks upon the blind
  And strikes their darkness deeper,

29

Which ever, from our birth,

    Leads down the deathward dances,

For hourly on the earth

    War casts its bayonet glances.

PEACE

I hear in the night the echoing trouble of
    multiple drums;
Flutes lift their piercing fountains; a shadowy
    army comes,
The soldiers, the sailors, the banners and the
    brave,
For we have had a victory and they have had a
    grave.

I see in clouds the martyrs who burn above the
    mire—
The flowerlike, the towerlike whom love led
    through the fire.
They die their deaths before me, beneath a
    broken sky;
They light earth's bloody pastures. I know their
    soundless cry:

"The house not made with hands once more is
overthrown;
The old men's vision failed, the young men's
dream has flown.
They turned upon their brothers, how shall they
atone?
Wake to the field below where they have slain
their own."

PROTHALAMIUM

(To a bride in war time)

Now the doom on land and sea
   Lengthens toward the wedding day,
Let the bridal bravely be
   Though the world should burn away.

Face, with phoenix wings unfurled,
   Deepening ashes, towering pyre.
Rise above a ruined world
   With a more than mortal fire.

Speed the mating, crown the vow
   While the brand of havoc gleams.
Now's the time to mate and now
   Breed the men with better dreams.

HEARD FROM A DARK STAGE

Two Voices

What's there?
               No stranger.
                     Who?
                           The ghost
Of the days you lived and lost.

What have I to do with you
When the night hours are so few?
Take away the cup you wreathe
With nettle. Leave me. Let me breathe.

These you planted long ago,
These the weeds and this the woe.
If the lips refuse to sip
I must make the weeds a whip.

Lash or poison then, but know
I shall be beyond the blow.

Pour the acid. Rain the rod.
Out of my wounds I flow to God.

Would you leave me lost, behind?
You have vision. I am blind.
If we mount to higher things,
I am the sleet upon the wings.

Shall I never, then, be free
And out of darkness grow to see,
Glowing ripe in sunny air,
The fruit that I was born to bear?

Never so, while nettle seed
Lifts no fruitage but a weed.

Deep then, in my broken earth
I'll bring other seed to birth.
Out of it I'll seize and shape
Life the vine, and love the grape.

35

In them, through those veins I'll pour
Myself, my being, to its core.
The vine of life, that twining gleam,
Shall bear me in its upward stream,
Bear my mind of fire and dream,
The burning fruit the fiery tide
From the heart within my side.
Fire to fire, I shall have passed
Free, triumphant at the last,
Rising, as the vine ascends,
Free, before the end of ends.

OUTLINE

There was longing on the beach.
    There were certain broken words
Mingled, to the end of speech,
    With the watersong of birds:

"Wait" and "yes," and he was gone.
    Distance waved a fading hem.
Then the shore she stood upon
    Faced the years that sundered them.

Back he came, the world-beguiled,
    To the sands where youth had clung.
But the shade that waited, smiled
    The smiling of the too long young.

SONGS FROM A STORY

How long is life on earth and time how fleeting
   Lovers that cling may learn at last with tears
When, in their utmost hour, they hear the
      beating
   Wings of the passage of a thousand years.

.   .   .

Whether the field-flower blossoms long and late
Or lays untimely down its colored freight,
Autumn will yield to all an equal fate.

"THE WORD THAT WALKED AMONG THE ANCIENT TREES"

—WILLIAM BLAKE, *Songs of Experience*

I

Night Song

In you alone has been our home and star,
Life, in all ages, risen from birth to birth,
Before the mountains leaped in their upcasting
Or ever you had uttered forth the earth
And, as a dream, the world, you were and are
From everlasting and to everlasting.

You turn man back to dust with his delight,
Saying, "Return to earth with other clay;
Return, O sons of men." For in your sight
A thousand years are but as yesterday,
A day, a dream, a watching in the night.

39

We are cut off. We are as dreams in flight.
We are like grass which meets the morning's face
With freshness. In the morning it is bright
But in the evening it has perished quite.
It is cut down and withers in its place.

For so your harvest finds and reaps us soon
And so your scythe of change cuts off our days.
Our flaws lie bare before you as at noon,
Our inmost thoughts before your presence blaze.

For all our days are ended in one fate,
Our time, our utmost years, a piteous stay.
Our years are like a cobweb wiped away
Or like a bitter pathway found too late,
Reaching through darkness where we grope and
     sigh
To the dark ending into which we fly.

The measure of your changes and their power,
Who knows it? Or the measure of our fear?

Waken us then as our brief days appear,

And bring the understanding heart to flower.

Return, O Life. How long will you be far?

Return. Lead up your children from this night

And through the gateways where your mornings
        are

That we may see and learn to bear the light.

Gladden us for the days when we were scorned,

The shadowy days that overflowed our cup,

For all these many days. O lift us up,

And for as many years as we have mourned.

And may the world that we have dreamed
        endure.

By after-comers let a light be caught

Out of your splendor. May your favor fall

Upon our world, your bounty on us all,

And make secure the work our hands have
        wrought;

Our handwork and our fruits, O make secure.

Adam's Song of the Visible World

Praise, O my heart, with praise from depth and
    height
To you, O Source of Life. How very great
The glories are that beat upon my sight
From you, so robed with honor and the weight
Of majesty, who clothe yourself with light
As with a garment, veiling you from us.

You stretch the heavens outward like a tent
And set the sky's pavilions upon beams
Under the waters; you have made and sent
The cloud to be your carrier as it streams
Upon the wings of winds; at your desire
Life woke and made the darkness glorious,
And man rose upward from the atom-fire.

You laid down the foundations of the earth
Not to be moved for ages from their place.

You raised the sea to cover all its girth
As under armor, and the waters stood
Upon the mountains over all its face.
At your rebuke they turned, they heeded well.
At your first thunder peal they fled and fell.

You set a bound against them and a shore
Not to be crossed and there the dry land first
Rose and the mountains rose and there between,
Each to its bed you made the valleys sink.
There fall the fountains which you made to pour
Among the hills, and there where it is green
Out of the field come all its beasts to drink,
And with them even the shyest quench their
      thirst.

Beside them all the birds of heaven live
Singing from branches. So your glory fills
Earth with the fruits of it, even as you give
Rain from your upper chambers to the hills.

You make the grass that grows for you to feed
The cattle, and you make the herbs abound
For all the beasts of man which serve his need,
So he may bring his food out of the ground
And bread to make his heart endure his toil,
And so that wine may rise up from the earth,
Lighting the heart of man and in his mirth
Making his face shine brighter than with oil.

The trees of Life are filled with dew and float
On the high hills, the cedars which you made
Where the birds build and nestle in the shade.
As for the stork, her house is in the fir.
In the high mountain refuge the wild goat
Finds pasture, and the coney homes for her,
Safe in the rock where she is not afraid.

You made the moon and gave to her a power
To keep the seasons measured with her light.
All day the sun has knowledge of his hour

For setting. And the darkness becomes night.

Then the wild beasts under the shadows lurk

And the young lions roar after their prey.

They seek from Life the meat they may devour.

When the sun rises, they all creep away,

Back to their dens, and crouch from any sight.

Man wakens and goes outward to his work

And to his burden till the end of day.

What life! What splendors in how many shapes

Are in this world, O Source, who made them all!

And with what wisdom made them, great and
        small!

Even their number on the earth escapes

Dreams or imaginings. The earth is full.

And yonder is the sea, how vast, how wide,

Flowing with living things innumerable,

The hugest and the hid, sharing the tide,

They that divide the wave, or sleepers curled.

There go the ships! There rolls leviathan

Whom you have formed to frolic in that world.

They wait on you alone, all beasts and man,

To have their food from you, and they are fed.

When your hand opens they are satisfied;

You give; they gather. When they think you far

A trouble comes upon them and a dread.

You take away their breath; they fade, they fall,

They go again to be the dust they tread.

You breathe upon the dust, they rise and are.

Your glory is forever and with dance

You move among your works and they to you.

You look upon the earth and at your glance

It sways with trembling and above the hills

A smoke ascends where you have touched their
      rest.

I will sing praises to you while life fills

My flesh with breath; as long as life shall stream

From you within me, I will sing your light.

May all my thought and all I dare in dream

Be true to you, acceptable and blest.

You are my tide of joy, my sea, my shore,

My field of sky with stars that never set,

And I will learn your wonders all my days,

Let me remember you in pain and let

The spirit of denial vanish quite

From earth and be forgotten in its ways,

And my blind ways in darkness be no more.

THE APPLES

Here in the May-bright square of the city he
  stood,

Young, on a morning that now seems a world
  away;

When the trees that he stared among seemed of
  an evil wood

With a silence coiled at the root, aimed straight at
  the day.

And he thought of a hillside orchard with bees
  asway

And he looked at the towers and thought they
  were better in sand,

Here where the gods he had sickened all year to
  obey

Portioned his breath and his dreams with a brute
  command,

Until he remembered with tears his father's hand.

And he looked in the people's eyes and he thought
  of hell

And he wondered at Whitman endlessly sound-
ing it all.

Could he have felt it as deeply, and known as well

Of the life-long sweat between the wolves and the
wall,

Or the sparrow and hawk upheld and the dove let
fall,

Or the ugly mask of the street with the smile of a
friend,

And the signs of the overfed beast each gilding a
stall?

For out of this ravin and ruin what wings could
ascend?

Enough. They had taken his dream and this was
the end.

Colorless? No, they shone like the fountain
there

With its poor mechanical leap at a giant's will.

But after the age-long heave, this moment of
air,—

Was it worthy the rainbow that martyrs had died
    to fulfill?
Or only to grind and be ground in an endless mill
With life run dry in winning the foremost place,
And a sneer at a god asleep on a far-off hill,
While over the thirsting seed on the desert's face
Hurtled the lightning of Time from the thunders
    of Space.

And he thought at last of a tale he had once heard
    told
Of a better place, on a golden shore of the sea,
Dim, where the dancers move under apples of
    gold,
Fruits of a happier earth, on a golden tree,
All day, in a world grown deathless, unsorrowful,
    free.
All night the gatherers lit by the apples would
    reap.
It was all in the story for nowhere else could it be;

The garden, the tides drifting into his mind from
    the deep.
And he sank on a stone of the fountain and fell
    asleep.

And suddenly there to the dreamer's vision a
    gleam
Rivered the air and he heard a song in the roar.
It came and went among leaves through branches
    of dream
And he heard the pitiful sound of the city no
    more.
For there in the street was the shining earth of the
    shore
And the walls of the street fell away to a long sea
    reach
And a bough was over his head and he saw what it
    bore,
For he stood in a golden shadow there on the
    beach
Under the apples of life, like a ripe world each.

And the gold hanging over its image of gold in
 the sea

Forever shone from the bough, and the young
 fruit grew

Forever, through fountains heard in the sound of
 the tree

Over the garden, and dancers moved in the dew

With words of a happier song than any he knew,

And the tree's least leaf gave light of a deeper
 kind

Than any ray of the sky that a bough let through,

And the shining fruit bore deeper sight in his
 mind,

For it shone on the people he thought he had left
 behind.

They seemed like people asleep whose eyelids lift

On the bitter paths of the blind all night
 unhealed;

To be there so near to the apples' deathless gift,

Whose boughs were over them all with life to
 yield,

And the gold ungathered from the branches'
  field:

So little gathered of all the skies had sown;

To be there and the dream so hidden, the
  fountain sealed.

But he seemed to himself there blinder than all
  he had known,

For he hadn't believed in the fruit and the shore
  was his own.

He remembered a sea-wind's lift in the sunny air,

And moved leaves wreathing fruit, as he took
  what he found.

But he felt the weight of the apple all he could
  bear

And he tasted it,—bitter,—and let it fall to the
  ground.

And the sea plunged once at the land a wave without sound,

And the shore was a gleam in a far-off surf's
  retreat,

And the street reclouded about him—the vision
  drowned.

But he wished for the apple again that had lain at
  his feet;

For the fruit was bitter at first but afterward
  sweet.

So he knew there was no escape at the world's end
  stored,

No escape in a sleep or beyond to a sea more vast,

But here where he breathed was the island,
  glittering-shored,

By the sound of whose waters the songs were a
  shadow cast.

And he saw at the street's end there how it deep-
  ened at last

Into the garden fed by the song and stream.

So his vision had brought one thing from the
  waves he had passed,

For his eyes held fast to the fire-like seed of his
  gleam;

He had brought that back for the fruit of a better
  dream.

LEGEND

When the wounded seaman heard the ocean
    daughters
  With their dreamy call
Lull the stormy demon of the waters,
  He remembered all.

He remembered knowing of an island charted,
  "Past a flying fire,"
Where a fruit was growing, winey-hearted,
  Called "the mind's desire."

Near him broke the stealing rollers into jewels
  Round a tree, and there
Sorrow's end and healing, peace, renewals
  Ripened in the air.

So he knew he'd found it and he watched the
    glory
  Burning on the tree

With the dancers round it—like the story—
   In the swinging sea.

Lovely round the honey-colored fruit, the
      motion
   Made a leafy stir.
Songs were in that sunny tree of ocean
   Where the apples were.

First the ocean sung them, then the daughters
      after,
   Dancing to the word.
Beauty danced among them with low laughter
   And the harp was heard.

In that sea's immeasurable music sounded
   Songs of peace, and still
From the bough the treasure hung down
      rounded
   To the seaman's will.

Redder than the jewel-seeded beach and sharper
    Were the wounds he bore,
Hearing, past the cruel dark, a harper
    Lulling on the shore.

Long he watched the wonders, ringed with
        lovely perils,
    Watched the apples gleam
In the sleepy thunders on the beryls,
    Then he breathed his dream:

"Bloody lands and flaming seas and cloudy
        slaughter,
    Hateful fogs unfurled,
Steely horror, shaming sky and water,
    These have wreathed the world.

"Give me fruit for freighting, till my anchor
        grapples
    Home, in harbor cast:
Earth shall end her hating through the apples
    And be healed at last."

Then the sea-girls, lifting up their lovely voices
    With the secret word,
Sang it through the drifting ocean noises
    And the sailor heard:

Ocean-old the answers reached his failing sinew,
    Touched, unveiled his eyes:
"Beach and bough and dancers are within you,
    There the island lies.

"Though the heavens harden, though the
        thunders hover,
    Though our song be mute,
Burning in our garden for the lover,
    Still unfolds the fruit."

Outward from that shore the happy sailor,
        turning,
    Passed the fleets of sleep,
Passed his pain and bore the secret, burning,
    Homeward to the deep.

MONOTONE TRIUMPHANT

Over and over her breast said,
"Cover me from rain and snowing;
I who was alive am dead,
He who has my life is going."

Somewhere in the room his tread
Halted and she rose at last;
Something more was being said,
Words to blunt the edge of knowing.

Scythelike, sweeping to the mowing,
Pity's tempered whisper sped;
Waste on waste her dreams lay cast
Where, at dawn, the worlds were growing.

Suddenly the dark was past.
High her pathway gleamed ahead:
Bridges of the lightning's thread

Bore her through the moonless vast
Safe above that steely flowing.

For her soul had cried aghast;
"If such dearth as mine be shed
Through the skies and all our sowing
Bring such desert at the last,
I myself must yield the bread,
Though the earth and heavens have passed
Hunger shall not find me fled;
Death shall find my spirit glowing,
Find my pastures greenly spread,
And the living streams unslowing."

THE SINGERS IN A CLOUD

Overhead at sunset all heard the choir.
Nothing could be seen except brighter grey
Raining beauty earthward, flooding with desire
All things that listened there in the broken day;
Songs from freer breathers, their unprisoned fire
Out of cloudy fountains, flying and hurled,
Fell and warmed the world.

Sudden came a wind and birds were laid bare,
Only music warmed them round their brown
       breasts.
They had sent the splendors pouring through
       the air,
Love was their heat and home far above their
       nests.
Light went softly out and left their voices there.
Starward passed for ever all that great cry,
Burning, round the sky.

On the earth the battles war against light,
Heavy lies the harrow, bitter the field.
Beauty, like a river running through the night,
Streams past the stricken ones whom it would
        have healed
But the darkened faces turn away from sight.
Blind, bewildered nations sow, reap, and fall,
Shadows gather all.

Far above the birdsong bright shines the gold,
Through the starry orchards earth's paths are
        hung;
As she moves among them glowing fruits unfold,
Such that the heavens there reawaken young.
Overhead is beauty, healing for the old
Overhead in morning, nothing but youth,
Only lovely youth.

SANTA BARBARA BEACH

Now while the sunset offers,
    Shall we not take our own:
The gems, the blazing coffers,
    The seas, the shores, the throne?

The sky-ships, radiant-masted
    Move out, bear low our way.
Oh, Life was dark while it lasted,
    Now for enduring day.

Now with the world far under,
    To draw up drowning men
And show them lands of wonder
    Where they may build again.

There earthly sorrow falters,
    There longing has its wage;
There gleam the ivory altars
    Of our lost pilgrimage.

—Swift flame—then shipwrecks only
　　Beach in the ruined light;
Above them reach up lonely
　　The headlands of the night.

A hurt bird cries and flutters
　　Her dabbled breast of brown;
The western wall unshutters
　　To fling one last rose down.

A rose, a wild light after—
　　And life calls through the years,
"Who dreams my fountain's laughter
　　Shall feed my wells with tears."

HEADLAND ORCHARDS

First Voice

April lit the apple flower and waved it,
    Music nested on the spray,
Loudly called the lookout bird through
        rainbows,
    Earth was curving into May.

In that hour the light from hillside orchards
    Pierced me, and the heavens about
Opened, and before intenser burning,
    Fire by fire my heart went out.

Flashing seas beyond the melted skymark
    Sang beneath another dome;
There my vision sailed to breathless knowledge,
    Sailed and found and drew back home.

Peace was in me from the starry motion,
    Then my breast received the sign;

At life's marriage feast the hidden lover,
Master of the water and the wine.

Through my flesh the suns of power and beauty
Warmed the moaning worlds to song;
Bread and healing from my broken body
Fed the sky-bewildered throng.

But the morning fell as leaves around me,
And the clay unpurified
Mocked me, scourged me, till the dove-like glory
Vanished from my wounded side.

Broken apple branches reaching sunward,
Distant sea and no sail spread,
These remained, and clouds above the hillside
And the multitude unfed.

Yet my heart had found on one far island
Where the high dream dipped its prow,

Arrowy odors of immortal apples,
  Raining from a golden bough.

Second Voice

I was with you, I have never left you.
  Through your breath I breathe the night,
Through your veins my pulses flow in darkness,
  But in deeper worlds is light.

Deep within you sweep the burning splendors
  Brighter than your gaze can bear;
There I watch among the dawns within you,
  Sky on sky is folded there.

There I see the outward heavens open
  As the inner heavens unfold;
There, in tidal light, eternal islands
  Orb the ever-living gold.

On those inward shores are fountains lifting
   Powers and suns of endless might;
Songs of birth and gleams of dancers dancing
   Wash the ripening worlds with light.

Wanderers deepening to those bright horizons
   Hidden by the body's wall,
Slowly as through music long forgotten
   Reach me and remember all.

Inward, past the shadows' reach, my light is,
   I am there whom tears conceal;
After victories I am in the stillness,
   Underneath despairs I heal.

He who finds me finds the sky above him
   Holds the weight of clouds no more,
But the common day another daylight
   And the sea of life a shore.

SURVIVORS

On a sea island's green and swaying world
Satiric Time heaps treasures, and the shore
Far to the waves echoes an old dismay,
For heavy along it certain moths lie curled;
Weapons and mouths they have, but little more,
And whosoever sees them, looks away.

Yet once that race envied the sky through tears;
And their mornings and their evenings grew
Until the mightiest flashed in wings of light,
Ravished with blood up from the creeping years
To beat against the floor of heaven and through,
And pour down daysprings gloriously bright.

Mad butterflies: that hour a wind prepared
Emptied the air of all, and they were drowned,
And the sea moaned that washed their icy wings.
But these the wingless, these who never dared,
Went warm and safe and fat upon the ground;
And later, in due season, put forth stings.

69

SEA DREAM

The blood of man varies somewhat from the sea water of today, but approaches even more closely in composition the primal ocean out of which human life arose.

—BIO-CHEMISTRY.

Sometimes at night a song comes flying
Among the shadowy fields in sleepers
Who waken to its sweet careering
Through their bodies' color and grace:
Magic pierces to their hearing
With sounds that are not heard by day;
Silence, breaking from its keepers,
Flies and music takes its place.
Those who waken and hear it crying
Find it beats with tidal motion;
It is the blood within their clay,
Remembering its ancient ocean.

To hear such wild and dreamy strains

Borne past the dim shores of the veins

The heart stops short—then beats again,

So to keep the singing flowing

Through the lands that lie in men.

For in the song those thousand streams

Are telling of their ancient fountain,

The sea, with all its jewels glowing

And beauty running on the waves,

Or buried in the water-mountain

Where the sea Shape, snowy and old,

In deeps that mock the diver's wish,

Blood-blind with war and a hate untold,

Still dooms and tombs in his diamond caves

The silver navies of the fish;

And the cold sea-worm, all curled

About the bones of battle gleams.

"Long past," (the song runs) , "left behind,

—But we remember all in dreams,—

The battles in the water world

Till the landward gates were passed.
Long since, all dim, long left behind,
The foes, the fangs, the hates at last
Buried in the water-mountain
With the nations of the blind."

Then the song changes and is young.
A new music leaps in birth,
Flying in the veins of each,
Flooding through the body's earth,
Telling with the spirit's tongue
Of new seas lifting on another beach.
In the spirit, in the heart's deep places,
Those hidden seas increase:
And lit with dawn from the eternal spaces
Break on the mind with surges soft as fleece;
Fill it in silence from a tidal fountain,
Until the coming day shall gleam
When the wells of hate are sealed,
Buried in the shining mountain

On the day of the heart's overflowing

When the earth is washed and healed,

And the lovers with the dream,

From ocean and to ocean going,

Shall lift at last into the living peace.

So the song tells, and much besides

Of glories in the blood's dim tides;

Much that no ear of dust can mark

Of marvels in the body's dark,

Singing of marvels in the body's dark.

EYE-WITNESS

Down by the railroad in a green valley
By dancing water, there he stayed awhile
Singing, and three men with him, listeners,
All tramps, all homeless reapers of the wind,
Motionless now and while the song went on
Transfigured into mages thronged with visions;
There with the late light of the sunset on them
And on clear water spinning from a spring
Through little cones of sand dancing and fading
Close beside pine woods where a hermit-thrush
Cast, when love dazzled him, shadows of music
That lengthened, fluting through the singer's
      pauses
While the sure earth rolled eastward bringing
      stars
Over the singer and the men that listened
There by the roadside, understanding all.

A car went by but nothing seemed to be changed.
Some eye among the passers must have flashed
Out to the singer, through the speeding window,
Carelessly bearing off the scene for ever,
With idle wonder what the men were doing,
Seeing they were so strangely fixed, and seeing
Torn papers from their smeary dreary meal
Spread on the ground with old tomato cans
Muddy with dregs of lukewarm chicory,
Neglected while they listened to the song.
And while he sang the singer's face was lifted,
And the sky shook down a soft light upon him
Out of its branches where like fruits there were
Many beautiful stars and planets moving,
With lands upon them, rising from their seas,
Glorious lands with glittering sands upon them,
With soils of gold and magic mould for seeding,
The shining loam of lands afoam with gardens
On mightier stars with giant rains and suns
There in the heavens; but on none of all

Was there ground better than he stood upon:
There was no world there in the sky above him
Deeper in promise than the earth beneath him
Whose dust had flowered up in him the singer
And three men understanding every word.

The Tramp Sings:

I will sing, I will go, and never ask me why.
I was born a rover and a passer-by.

I seem to myself like water and sky,
A river and a rover and a passer-by.

But in the winter three years back
We lit us a night fire by the track,

And the snow came up and the fire it flew
And we couldn't find the warming room for two.

One had to suffer, so I left him the fire
And I went to the weather from my heart's desire.

It was night on the line, it was no more fire,
But the zero whistle through the icy wire.

As I went suffering through the snow
Something like a shadow came moving slow.

I went up to it and I said a word;
Something flew above it like a kind of bird.

I leaned in closer and I saw a face;
A light went round me but I kept my place.

My heart went open like an apple sliced;
I saw my Saviour and I saw my Christ.

Well, you may not read it in a book,
But it takes a gentle Saviour to give a gentle look.

I looked in his eyes and I read the news;
His heart was having the railroad blues.

Oh, the railroad blues will cost you dear,
Keeps you moving on for something that you
don't see here.

We stood and whispered in a kind of moon;
The line was looking like May and June.

I found he was a roamer and a journey man,
Looking for a lodging since the night began.

He went to the doors but he didn't have the pay,
He went to the windows, then he went away.

Says: "We'll walk together and we'll both be fed."
Says: "I will give you the 'other' bread."

Oh, the bread he gave and without money!
O drink, O fire, O burning honey!

It went all through me like a shining storm:
I saw inside me, it was light and warm.

78

I saw deep under and I saw above,
I saw the stars weighed down with love.

They sang that love to burning birth,
They poured that music to the earth.

I heard the stars sing low like mothers.
He said: "Now look, and help feed others."

I looked around, and as close as touch
Was everybody that suffered much.

They reached out, there was darkness only;
They could not see us, they were lonely.

I saw the hearts that deaths took hold of,
With the wounds bare that were not told of;

Hearts with things in them making gashes;
Hearts that were choked with their dreams' ashes;

Women in front of the rolled-back air,
Looking at their breasts and nothing there;

Good men wasting and trapped in hells;
Hurt lads shivering with the fare-thee-wells.

I saw them as if something bound them;
I stood there but my heart went round them.

I begged him not to let me see them wasted.
Says: "Tell them then what you have tasted."

Told him I was weak as a rained-on bee;
Told him I was lost.—Says: "Lean on me."

Something happened then I could not tell,
But I knew I had the water for every hell.

Any other thing it was no use bringing;
They needed what the stars were singing,

What the whole sky sang like waves of light,
The tune that it danced to, day and night.

Oh, I listened to the sky for the tune to come;
The song seemed easy, but I stood there dumb.

The stars could feel me reaching through them;
They let down light and drew me to them.

I stood in the sky in a light like day,
Drinking in the word that all things say

Where the worlds hang growing in clustered
        shapes
Dripping the music like wine from grapes.

With "Love, Love, Love," above the pain,
—The vinelike song with its winelike rain.

Through heaven under heaven the song takes root
Of the turning, burning, deathless fruit.

I came to the earth and the pain so near me,
I tried that song but they couldn't hear me.

I went down into the ground to grow,
A seed for a song that would make men know.

Into the ground from my roamer's light
I went; he watched me sink to night.

Deep in the ground from my human grieving,
His pain ploughed in me to believing.

Oh, he took earth's pain to be his bride,
While the heart of life sang in his side.

For I felt that pain, I took its kiss,
My heart broke into dust with his.

Then sudden through the earth I found life
        springing;
The dust men trampled on was singing.

Deep in my dust I felt its tones;
The roots of beauty went round my bones.

I stirred, I rose like a flame, like a river,
I stood on the line, I could sing for ever.

Love had pierced into my human sheathing,
Song came out of me simple as breathing.

A freight came by, the line grew colder.
He laid his hand upon my shoulder.

Says, "Don't stay on the line such nights,"
And led me by the hand to the station lights.

I asked him in front of the station-house wall
If he had lodging. Says: "None at all."

I pointed to my heart and looked in his face.—
"Here,—if you haven't got a better place."

He looked and he said: "Oh, we still must roam
But if you'll keep it open, well, I'll call it 'home'."

The thrush now slept whose pillow was his wing.
So the song ended and the four remained
Still in the faint starshine that silvered them,

While the low sound went on of broken water

Out of the spring and through the darkness

    flowing

Over a stone that held it from the sea.

Whether the men spoke after could not be told,

A mist from the ground so veiled them, but they

    waited

A little longer till the moon came up;

Then on the gilded track leading to the

    mountains,

Against the moon they faded in common gold

And earth bore East with all toward the new

    morning.

THREE O'CLOCK

(Morning)

The jewel-blue electric flowers
 Are cold upon their iron trees.
Upraised, the deadly harp of rails
 Whines for its interval of ease.
The stones keep all their daily speech
 Buried, but can no more forget
Than would a water-vacant beach
 The hour when it was wet.

A whitened few wane out like moons,
 Ghastly from some torn edge of shade;
A drowning one, a reeling one,
 And one still loitering after trade.
On high the candor of a clock
 Portions the dark with solemn sound.
The burden of the bitten rock
 Moans up from underground.

Far down the street a shutting door
Echoes the yesterday that fled
Among the days that should have been
Which people cities of the dead.
The banners of the steam unfold
Upon the towers to meet the day;
The lights go out in red and gold
But time goes out in gray.

THE SON

I heard an old farm-wife,
    Selling some barley,
Mingle her life with life
    And the name "Charley."

Saying: "The crop's all in,
    We're about through now;
Long nights will soon begin,
    We're just us two now.

"Twelve bushel at sixty cents,
    It's all I carried—
He sickened making fence;
    He was to be married—

"It feels like frost was near—
    His hair was curly.
The spring was late that year,
    But the harvest early."

87

THE FEASTERS

I

Pioneers and Indians

From the waters of the east
Came a people bleak and eager,
Sailor, priest and stern beleaguer,
Sailing meagre to the feast
From the waters of the east.

"Leave the hunger to the least,"—
And their hosts were least among them.
So the bitter crust they flung them
And they sung them, when they ceased,
"Leave the hunger to the least."

Toward the waters of the west
Went a people few and lonely,
Having now their hunger only,

Going lonely on their quest
Toward the waters of the west.

Watch them only, it is best;
Gods and lovers, men and daughters
Dumbly toward the west sea waters
Swept, to let the ancient breast
Find the banquet and the guest.

II

Mexican Plunder

Toward the river in the south
Feasting fingers reach to battle;
Glide and rattle in the drouth
Toward the fats that follow battle;
Oils and ores and desert cattle;
Sweet to feed a feasting mouth,
Past the river in the south.

So the children of the sun,
With the feasters' fingers near them
At the stream, have learned to fear them
When they hear them reach and run
Toward the morsels one by one,
Toward the ores and oils that smear them,
Toward the gardens of the sun.

When their doom is not far off,
Then the feasters' faiths grow hollow.
When their leaders turn and follow
From their wallow by the trough,
When they march, through raving hours,
Breeding war to bear them dreams,
When the nightmare foals with screams,
Rolling on the bloody flowers,
When a death shall save a trough,
Then the doom is not far off.

THE BIRD AND THE TREE

Blackbird, blackbird in the cage,
There's something wrong tonight.
Far off the sheriff's footfall dies,
The minutes crawl like last year's flies
Between the bars, and like an age
The hours are long tonight.

The sky is like a heavy lid
Out here beyond the door tonight.
What's that? A mutter down the street.
What's that? A sound of yells and feet.
For what you didn't do or did
You'll pay the score tonight.

No use to reek with reddened sweat,
No use to whimper and to sweat.
They've got the rope; they've got the guns,
They've got the courage and the guns;

And that's the reason why tonight;
No use to ask them any more.
They'll fire the answer through the door—
You're out to die tonight.

There where the lonely cross-road lies,
There is no place to make replies;
But silence, inch by inch, is there,
And the right limb for a lynch is there;
And a lean daw waits for both your eyes,
Blackbird.

Perhaps you'll meet again some place.
Look for the mask upon the face:
That's the way you'll know them there—
A white mask to hide the face:
And you can halt and show them there
The things that they are deaf to now,
And they can tell you what they meant—
To wash the blood with blood. But how
If you are innocent?

Blackbird singer, blackbird mute,

They choked the seed you might have found.

Out of a thorny field you go—

For you it may be better so—

And leave the sowers of the ground

To eat the harvest of the fruit,

Blackbird.

THE WINTER CRYSTAL

In the night, at the sound of winter thunder,
As I brooded upon my wounded planet,
Broken rain from the gulf upon my window
Passed down shadowy ways and there was silence.

Moon on moon from a cloud of vanished Aprils
Lit my heart with a dream of springs remem-
      bered,
Till alone of the year's four worlds of wonder
Spring seemed tender and I forgot the others.

When grass rises again (I thought) the sorrow
Will lie hidden forever under beauty;
So I longed for the time of apple blossoms,
All my dreams were upon the blowing lilacs.

But some whirlwind that held the winter's secret
Rose and lifting the frozen days as curtains

Showed me Time as an upper sky of crystal
Flushed with images yet to be reflected.

There past lightnings I saw the coming season
Fill with shapes of the things to be unfolded;
But no healing was there; I saw none solaced,
Saw no comfort uplifted by the snowdrop.

Nothing beautiful rose but close above it
Shadows thwarted its mercy for the gazer.
By the crocus and by the valley-lily
Stood the sorrowful, stood the broken-hearted.

There I saw but I could not reach the children,
Saw them taste of the grindings of their labor,
Saw behind them the granite eyes of hunger,
All was barren as ever in the winter.

And I thought that I heard life crying round me,
All about me its voice in winter crying:

"I am flowerless, fruitless, for love has left me,
I am nothing without his breath to warm me.

"He who left me was mine among the lilies
Timeless dawnings before these heavens
       gathered.
There he found me and sealed me his forever,
There I gave him the worlds unstained, un-
       warring.
Whom I call and desire until the daybreak."

And I knew, if the golden spring comes loveless,
Earth shall wait but the bitter moons flow empty.
Though old mockeries plant the thorny truces,
All the fruitage of steel repose has fallen.

Only weaponless, all-forgiving, tender,
Earth shall darken the skies no more with anguish,
But with music and light shall move among them
When the lands shall be only love-defended.

Dove-low waters among the kindled willows
Then would lift to anoint a dust unsaddened,

Piercing cries of the spirit from the marshes

Melt with chorusings echoed from the hillsides.

Harplike mysteries called through glowing
   orchards,

Shy, invisible laughters from the thickets,

All that uttered the dream while earth turned
   heedless

Then with freshets of song would cool its fever.

Unbelievably then would life inhabit

All green places within the heart, outpouring

Spring with thunder of all her myriad fountains

In one cup for the healing of the nations.

Till in visionings all, as on a mountain,

Would with trembling, above the fallen
   blindness,

See how earth could be brighter than the sun-
   light,

Rayed with dreams, and above the treading glory,

Into opening heavens the song ascending.

THRENODY

AT THE HUNTING SEASON

In the middle of August when the southwest wind
Blows after sunset from the upper air
And through the dusk, Antares toward the west
Leads down the smouldering Scorpion to his lair.
After the longer days have crossed the sky
And left new sadness on the evening shores,
When the loud pageant of the year's high noon
Hints of the hour when it shall fade and fly,
Late summer nights begin to wander by
With one more hour for darkness or the moon.
On one of these, a night of griefs unguessed,
Life would not let me rest
But with low voices called me out of doors.

And then I saw and heard—
Multitudes, multitudes, under the moon they
    stirred!
The weaker children of our earthly breed;

Watchmen of whom our safety takes no heed;

Swift helpers of the wind that sowed the seed

Before the first field was or any fruit;

Warriors against the bivouac of the weed;

Earth's earliest ploughmen for the groping root,

All came about my head and at my feet

Bewildered, driven, hiding, fluttering, mute.

And I looked on and saw them one by one

Pass and become as nothing in the night.

Clothed smooth with red they were who once
were white;

Drooping, who once led armies to the sun,

Of whom the grass now topped the flight;

In scarlet now who once were brave in brown;

Climbers and builders of the silent town,

Creepers and burrowers all in crimson dye,

Winged mysteries of song that from the sky

Once dashed long music down.

And who would take away music from the earth?

Have we so much? Or love upon the hearth?

No more—the vision faded.

The trees that shelter life from birth to birth

Groaned upward, and the night wind's hoarse
  rebuff

Swept back the boughs and left the guilt
  unshaded.

Shall Nature's last-left refuge be invaded?

Has she not borne enough?

Now that the mirroring woodland pools begin to
  con her,

And her sad immemorial passion comes upon
  her,

Must the unfailing heavens overhead

Look down on still more pain and earth still hold

Wings newly broken or the fliers dead

Or see the woods and meadows that were gold

Redden and the leaves go redder to the mould

Beneath the dead or desperate feet

Of those who in next summer's meadows shall
  not meet?

Who has not seen in the high gulf of light

What, lower, was a bird, but now

Is moored and altered quite

Into an island of unshaded joy?

To whom the mate below upon the bough

Shouts once and brings him from the height—

Yet speeding and remembering the cloud

And the bright light he left, burning aloud,

He took a little of the day,

A little of the colored sky,

And of the joy that would not stay

He wove a song that cannot die.

Then, the unfathomable shame;

The one last wrong burned upward from the
        flame,

The watcher listened and the death was hurled

Bidding love once more beware,

Bringing one more loneliness on the world,

And one more darkness to the air.

Even the wind that all year loud or low

Somewhere upon the earth goes wandering,

That moaned and seemed to know,

The wind might tell in its unmortal tongue

Of what it moved among.

Even the wind might tell

Of those who wakened to the early light

And saw the day all Indian Summer-bright

And crept upstream through wood or field or
    brake

Only to find and take

The crumbs that from the master's table fell,

And of the thronging thunders that they met

And of the dew that made the grass blades wet,

Of how man's eyes grow blinder even as they

Who on these dawns are fire, at dusk are clay.

What shall be done

By you, who end so, heart by heart:

You for whose fate such fate forever hovers?

Singers and lovers,

If you would still have nests beneath the sun

Gather your broods about you and depart

Before the stony forward-pressing faces

Into the lands empty of any sound,

The more compassionate desert places.

Give men no more in winter the delight

To know that underneath the frozen ground

The warm life waits with never-uttered lore.

Take from our eyes the glory of great flight,

And let us see no more

People untroubled by a Fate's veiled eyes.

Leave us and leave the world forlorn.

No more high echoes from the skies

Of song's long utmost heavenward endeavor,

But let the silence pour on us for ever

The arrows of unutterable scorn.

Nor shall the cry of famine be a shield

Behind whose front a brutish mood would hide.

Stains, stains upon the lintels of our doors

Wait to be justified.

Shall there be mutterings at the season's yield?
Has eye of man seen bare the granary floors?
Are the fields wasted? Spilled the oil and wine?
Is the fat seed under the ground decayed?
Does the fig tree ever fail us or the vine?
Whose eyes have seen the harvest promise fade?
Or earth's last orchard heavy with fruit asway
Withered away?
No, not these things, but grosser things than these
Are the dim parents of a guilt not dim;
Ancestral urges out of old caves blowing,
When fear watched at our coming and our going
The horror of the chattering face of whim!
Hates, cruelties still following from the trees
To which we clung with hearts too dark for love,
Shames we have had all time to rid us of,
Outworn enslavements, blood-thirst never slaked,
Recalled, revived, and waked,
Unmeaning quarrels, and the clutch and thrust
Of snarling greeds from our old home, the dust.

Yet even of these one saving shape may rise;

Fear may unveil our eyes.

For who may know what curse would follow hard

Upon a land bare of the faithful races

Who day and night keep watch and guard

Over the treasure of the planted spaces?

Then the dry locust would lay waste his fill

And the blind worm lay tithe,

The unfed stones rot in the listless mill,

The sound of grinding cease.

No bending gold would whisper to the scythe,

Hunger at last would prove us of one blood,

The shores of dream be drowned in tides of need.

Horribly then the earth would be at peace,

The burden of the grasshopper indeed

Weigh down the green corn and the tender bud,

The plague of Egypt fall upon the wheat

And the shrill nit would batten in the heat.

EVENSONG

Beauty calls and gives no warning,

Shadows rise and wander on the day.

In the twilight, in the quiet evening

We shall rise and smile and go away.

Over the flaming leaves

Freezes the sky.

It is the season grieves,

Not you, not I.

All our springtimes, all our summers,

We have kept the longing warm within.

Now we leave the after-comers

To attain the dreams we did not win.

O we have wakened here and had our birth,

And that's the end of earth;

And we have toiled and smiled and kept
   the light,

And that's the end of night.

CEREMONY FOR BIRTH
AND NAMING

The parents or sponsors shall present themselves
with the child before the Speaker, who shall say:

In all this world of visible images
There is no music, neither shadow of sound
Nor gladness nor a glory to be found
Able to yield us, out of loveliness,
The life we dream, the breath that we pursue.
But still returns the dreamer to the day;
The child again, the morning strength to woo
Out of the over and the under heaven
The song that from our wearier reach withdrew;
The dawn returns, the ancient dark is driven
Forward and from the silence rolls the stone away.

Consider well your ways and lives,
You gardeners of the precious seed.
As brief attenders of the need,

Draw honey from the upper hives,
Make sweet the weather for the flower;
Withdraw the bonds and set it free.
You shall be watchers for an hour,
But it shall never cease to be.

I ask therefore:
Will you be mindful of your care,
Knowing you are, through him, of those
Who leave their colors in the air
When you are dust and he a rose?

(The parent answers)

Speaker:

Will you take thought before you find
The words to curb his longing will,
And from commands awhile be still,
Considering which of you is blind?

108

(The parent answers)

Speaker:

And who shall say what he must be
Who by your folly may not fly
Or, long be hindered from the sky
Or, shore-bound, never know the sea?

Make him the keeper of the key
To lock or hold in stern array
The urgent fiber of his clay
And send his ranging spirit free.

In the three names of Love, Light, and your
Divine Humanity I name you—

PAEAN FOR THE BODY'S PASSING

To the glowing feast of birth
All the distant guests return;
Nothing pauses in the earth.
But onward, where no temporal eye may range,
The lover and the love shall burn—
On the steadfast dreams ascending
Upward, through the widening halls of change,
To the banquet never ending.
And the wanderer ever young—
Flying toward the flying light—
Shall find the ripened worlds outflung
Upon the tables of his might.
All that slowly rose and globed and swayed
On the laddered vines of his endeavor
Shall be gathered up at last and weighed,
Gathered, pressed and poured with songs for ever.
Golden apples of fulfillment there,
Seeds to plant for those who rise thereafter,

Iron bowls of holy labor bear
Between the lamps of gorgeous laughter.
Never shall the revel fade
Nor the passing song be sung.

Though now the brief pavilion of our day
Fades as we climb to build the unfinished wall,
Though now no autumn orchard, yielding all,
Fulfills the flowers of May,
Yet on the pinions of immortal yearning,
Beyond the shadow of the unreturning,
Above the star that gives us wise forewarning
How wide the dusk enrings the steadfast light,
We shall renew and gather and requite,
We shall pursue and seize again the morning,
And be found no more by night.

Though from the evening to the morning glowing
No world may rise nor orbit-song be clear,
Where deeper need is shall be deeper knowing,

Where music hides there shall be ears to hear.
Down from the arches of dream a thunder of
       wings
Rolls, and for ever along the inward sight,
Out of the cloud and fear,
With all the heavens rushing earthward, armed,
A lightning plunging from the homes of light
Hints to the spirit that it stands unharmed.
And over all, beacons the face afar
Of the stern justice, weighing our desire,
Sifting the will-to-be from what we are,
Balancing longing with the longed-for fire,
Hunger with food, thirst with unfaltering springs,
Hope with the hope fulfilled, and with the night,
       a star.

Who has not left a dark abode
At noon, upon swift errands bent,
And stared along a blazing road
Sightless, till the pulsing veils were rent

That wisely waved him from the heart of light.
So with radiance overflowed,
The earthly vision faints with sight
And shall, till all grows clear with seeing
And all may know through fading night
That what was seen here shall not cease from
        being.
As a great circle, widening in the sea,
Passes forever to the shore, so we!
And if no coast appear nor any beach,
The spirit still will wander undefeated;
With battles and with new embracings, each
An endless circle endlessly completed.

Nothing shall be lost nor fall
From the winter-dreaming tree
But shall find another bough
And fly in other summers free.
Endless springs have kept the vow.
Here the spheral secret learn:

One has vanished into all;
All in one shall later burn
Outward from the dust.

                  And now,
As seed to wait the seed's recall,
Return.

Not from the shore may any requiem swell
Nor winging of farewell
From us within the bubble Time or Place;
We are already on the water's face,
And wave with wave shall endlessly ally,
Too near for need of summons or recall.
The end of earth is the beginning sky;
The sea is under all,
From whose unfathomed wells we rise and flow
Slowly along a winding glory, seeing
The wise unrest from which we had our being
And the ineffable to which we go.

TO CHILDREN

INVITATION

Arvia, east of the morning,
  Before the daylight grayed,
I heard a night song's warning:
  "This bubble-world shall fade.

"The daytime with its fire-flower,"
  It sang, "shall fade and stray;
And beauty, like a brier-flower,
  Shall pass—shall pass away."

Then soon the faint and far light
  Would fade beyond a beam
And we'd lie down without starlight
  And there would be no dream.

But now, when the noon is bluest,
  Like a shell that murmurs all,
I see this world is the truest
  Of any I recall.

The sky's wild birds are glancing,
    The sea's long waves are slow;
It's all a place for dancing
    But no one seems to know.

Come with me to the meadows,
    We'll dance your secret name
With an outside dance in shadows
    And an inside dance in flame.

The songs and the wings have slanted
    And blow with a golden sound;
Life burns like a peak enchanted,
    Oh wild, enchanted, crowned.

All day, while songs from the height fall,
    We'll dance the valleys bright,
But we'll be on the hills at nightfall
    In the lovely, lonely light.

.　　.　　.

Let's play we are a tune
And make a kind of song
About the sun and moon
Before the stars were born.
You be the breath, I'll be the horn,
It will not take us long.

JEAN SINGING

Lavender's blue in the garden,
 Lavender's bright.
When I am blind, my Beloved,
 You shall have sight.

I shall be dust in the garden,
 Deep from the storm.
You shall be shining still then,
 You shall be warm.

When I am hidden in shadow
 Under the years,
Call to me, tell me of all things
 Here among tears.

I shall remember the glory
 Filling this place,
The firebird calling through the rainbow:
 "Lift up your face."

I shall remember how beauty
  Over death, over birth,
Bridges a streaming music
  Here on the earth.

Only if wounds and the sorrow
  Made by men's hands
Still should outdeepen the waters,
  Darken the lands,

Even though you should recall me
  Then with your gleam,
I shall remember and turn me
  Back to my dream.

Q 7